WASHINGTON, D.C.

A PHOTOGRAPHIC PORTRAIT

PHOTOGRAPHY BY RANDY SANTOS

NARRATIVE BY SUSAN DIRANIAN

TWIN LIGHTS PUBLISHERS, ROCKPORT, MASSACHUSETTS

Copyright © 2014 by
Twin Lights Publishers, Inc.

All rights reserved. No part of this book may be reproduced in any form without written permission of the copyright owners. All images in this book have been reproduced with the knowledge and prior consent of the artists concerned and no responsibility is accepted by producer, publisher, or printer for any infringement of copyright or otherwise, arising from the contents of this publication. Every effort has been made to ensure that credits accurately comply with information supplied.

First published in the United States of America by:

Twin Lights Publishers, Inc.
51 Broadway
Rockport, Massachusetts 01966
Telephone: (978) 546-7398
www.twinlightspub.com

ISBN: 978-1-934907-20-7

10 9 8 7 6 5

(opposite)
WW II Memorial

(frontispiece)
U.S. Capitol

(jacket front)
U.S. Capitol

(jacket back, clockwise from top)
Jefferson Memorial, Supreme Court, Korean War Memorial

Book design by:
SYP Design & Production, Inc.
www.sypdesign.com

Printed in China

There is no city in the world quite like our nation's capital. It's a place where history meets modern day, power meets compromise, conflict meets peace. It's vibrant, peaceful, political, cultural, sensational, livable and wonderful. From the marble steps of the U.S. Capitol building and the White House to the monumental monuments and museums to the tranquil neighborhoods and parks, it's all captured in this detailed photographic portrait.

Located along the Potomac and Anacostia rivers, Washington, D.C. was planned to become the nation's capital. Named after our first president, Washington picked this particular location for its close proximity to established port towns, such as Georgetown and Alexandria, as well as to help form a compromise between the northern and southern states.

Pierre Charles L'Enfant and Benjamin Banneker worked together to create the look of this bold new capital. Inspired by historical architecture and styles, Washington, D.C. soon began to resemble L'Enfant's native France with its sweeping boulevards, uniquely structured buildings and its well-manicured grounds. In 1901, Congress established a special committee to help further implement L'Enfant's original plan and soon the monuments and the National Mall were established.

Many of the city's memorials and monuments have been ranked as America's most favorite architecture by the American Institute of Architects, including the U.S. Capitol building, Lincoln Memorial, Vietnam Veterans Memorial, Thomas Jefferson Memorial and the National Cathedral. Neighborhoods, such as Adams Morgan, Chinatown and Dupont Circle, exemplify the vibrancy and diversity found throughout D.C. The surrounding landscape, such as the cherry blossoms, reminds visitors and residents of the sheer beauty found in our nation's capital.

Take a look at what makes Washington, D.C. so wonderful. These stunning photographs will carry you inside D.C.'s most storied buildings, institutions, memorials, monuments, and landmarks and help make clear that there really is no other place in the world quite like our nation's capital.

U. S. Capitol *(opposite)*

The symbol of the United States and its people, the United States Capitol building sits on approximately 274 acres of land and features a variety of lawns, walkways, monumental sculptures and memorials, gardens, planinting areas, and fountains.

Architectural Landscape *(above)*

Originally a wooded wilderness, the grounds of the United States Capitol now feature a park-like setting with benches, fountains, gardens, and modern-day architectural landscaping known as "hardscapes." These magnificent structures add beauty and allure while also providing a secure perimeter around the property.

Ulysses S. Grant Memorial *(opposite)*

Located west of the U.S. Capitol building, the Ulysses S. Grant Memorial features the Civil War general and future president sitting on horseback as if observing a battle. Bronze sculptures of marching soldiers lie on opposite sides and four bronze lions lay still around the base of the memorial.

Rotunda (opposite)

The Rotunda stands 180 feet tall and 96 feet wide and features eight framed historical paintings, four wreathed panels, the portrait busts of historical explorers, including Christopher Columbus and Sir Walter Raleigh, as well as the Apotheosis of Washington, a true fresco painting by Constantino Brumidi.

National Statuary Hall (top)

Statues of former presidents and historical figures line the interior perimeter of the Rotunda including George Washington, Abraham Lincoln, Dwight D. Eisenhower, Thomas Jefferson and Dr. Martin Luther King, Jr. as well as pioneers of the woman suffrage movement Lucretia Mott, Elizabeth Cady Stanton, and Susan B. Anthony.

Fresco (bottom)

The *Apotheosis of Washington* features the spirit of George Washington rising to heaven on the arms of two women believed to represent Liberty and Victory/Fame. The former president is also surrounded by six groups of figures. The stunningly beautiful artwork spans across 4,664 square feet.

National Mall

Recognized as America's front yard, the National Mall spans over two miles and is home to many memorials and monuments including the Washington Monument, Lincoln Memorial, Vietnam Veterans Memorial, National World War II Memorial, Korean War Veterans Memorial, and the District of Columbia War Memorial.

Senate Fountain

Completed in 1932, the fountain features a hexagonal shape with multiple high jets of water extending out from its center. Water flows from lion-head spouts into a scalloped stone rim, which flows into a larger basin. Underwater lights change colors throughout a 20-minute cycle.

Freedom *(opposite)*

Resting atop the U.S. Capitol, the bronze *Statue of Freedom* features a woman in classical dress holding a sword in one hand and a laurel wreath of victory in the other. She stands on a cast-iron pedestal with the words *E Pluribus Unum* (Out of many, one) scripted along the base.

Peace Monument *(above)*

The monument at Peace Circle features two women, Grief and History, who mourn over the loss of life during the Civil War. The tablet that History holds is inscribed with the words, "They died that their country might live." Below stands another woman, Victory, with the infant Mars and Neptune resting besides her.

Capitol Fountain

A simple fountain located in the west plaza of the U.S. Capitol, the surrounding well-manicured grounds feature seasonal plants and trees and offer a picturesque and park-like contrast to the building's ornate architecture and structure.

Capitol Visitors Center

Located underneath the grounds of the U.S. Capitol building, the U.S. Capitol Visitors Center spans nearly 580,000 square feet and features interactive exhibits, two orientation theaters, an auditorium, visitor services including a restaurant, coat check and gift shops, and office space for House and Senate members.

White House

Recognized as the official residence and primary workspace of the President, the White House has been the home of every president since John Adams. The location of the White House was selected by George Washington in 1791. The property features 132 rooms, 35 bathrooms, and 6 levels in the residential area.

Twilight *(above)*

Also known as the Executive Office of the President of the United States, the White House is documented as a National Heritage Site and administered by the National Park Service. The property includes 18 acres of land and features the North and South Lawn, Jacqueline Kennedy Garden, and a rose garden.

Springtime *(right)*

Each year, the D.C. area celebrates the gift of 3,000 cherry trees from Mayor Yukio Ozaki of Tokyo in 1912. The National Cherry Blossom Festival features a variety of family-friend events including a kite festival, interactive educational events, food and drink tastings, fireworks, a parade, concerts, cherry blossom tours, and more.

Lincoln Memorial *(above)*

Located across from the Washington Monument, the Lincoln Memorial features the former president sitting within a Greek Doric temple with double wreath medallions and the names of the 36 states in the Union at the time of Lincoln's death. The memorial also features the inscription of Lincoln's well-known speeches.

Interior *(left and opposite)*

The interior of the memorial features inscriptions from Lincoln's second inaugural address and his Gettysburg Address. Ornate sculptures including eagles, wreaths and fasces surround the inscriptions and a large mural painting depicting the governing principles in Lincoln's life, including Freedom, Liberty, Justice and Law, is featured in the interior.

Sunrise Aboard Marine One

Operated by the HMX-1 Nighthawks squadron, the President flies home aboard *Marine One*. More than 800 Marines supervise the presidential fleet of helicopters. The helicopters are used to transport the president quickly and safely. As an added security measure, the helicopters fly in fleets of three or more.

Adaptation of the Pantheon (top)

Located on the shore of the Tidal Basin in West Potomac Park, the Thomas Jefferson Memorial features neoclassical architecture and borrows features from the Pantheon and Jefferson's residence, Monticello. A park-like setting surrounds the memorial including plants, shrubs, and cherry blossom trees.

Jefferson Memorial (bottom)

The Thomas Jefferson Memorial is a testament to our nation's quest for liberty and fairness for all. He is recognized as a spokesman for democracy, politically opposed slavery, and helped put an end to the international trading of slaves. Thomas Jefferson is also known as one of the country's greatest presidents.

Interior (opposite)

The interior of the memorial features numerous quotes from the former president, including the Preamble to the Declaration of Independence and other quotes involving religious freedom, notes on the state of Virginia, and letters to political leaders and diplomats such as George Washington and George Wythe.

Washington Monument *(above)*

Made of marble, granite and bluestone gneiss, the Washington Monument once stood partially finished for more than 20 years due to a lack of funds. Although construction resumed in 1876, the stone used never entirely matched. As a result, there is a distinct difference between the two construction phases.

Tidal Basin *(opposite)*

A partially man-made reservoir, the Tidal Basin sits between the Potomac River and the Washington Channel. Surrounded by memorials, including those dedicated to George Washington, Martin Luther King, Jr., Franklin D. Roosevelt and George Mason, the Tidal Basin is also home to the National Cherry Blossom Festival.

First Division Memorial *(above)*

Located in President's Park, the First Division Memorial was built by World War I veterans and dedicated to the lives lost in the war. The monument features two wings dedicated to the lives lost during World War II and the Vietnam War as well as a plaque dedicated to the lives lost during the Gulf War.

Victory *(left)*

Standing atop the 35-foot-tall column of the First Division Memorial is the gilded bronze statue of Victory. The initial design of the statue was criticized for not being sufficiently spiritual. Sculptor Daniel Chester French and architect Cass Gilbert worked diligently to rework the design of the statue to what it is today.

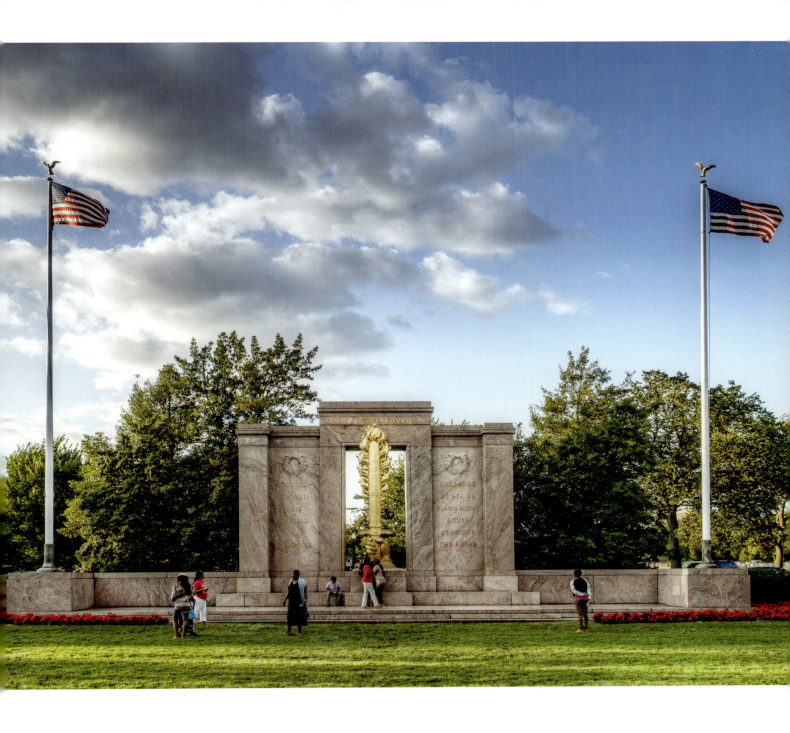

Second Division Memorial

The Second Division Memorial is dedicated to those who served in the Second Infantry Division during World War I. The monument also features two wings dedicated to the lives lost during World War II and the Korean War. The flaming sword symbolizes the defense of Paris from the Germans.

Marine Corps War Memorial

A photograph comes to life. Sculptor Felix de Weldon transformed an iconic photograph from World War II into a hauntingly beautiful, life-sized bronze sculpture better known as the Iwo Jima Memorial. The sculpture is dedicated to the men and women of the Marines who lost their lives defending our freedom.

WWII Memorial

The World War II Memorial consists of 56 granite pillars representing all 50 states as well as U.S. territories, a pair of arches on opposite ends inscribed with the words "Atlantic" and "Pacific," respectfully, and the Freedom Wall, which displays a gold star for every 100 lives lost during the war.

Navy Memorial (above)

The Navy Memorial honors those who serve, or have served, in the Navy, Marine Corps, Coast Guard, and the Merchant Marine. It features a ceremonial amphitheater, fountains, and pools depicting key moments in sea services. Made from artifacts from eight Navy ships, *The Lone Sailor* is located near the edge of the plaza.

Naval Heritage Center (opposite)

The Naval Heritage Center displays the history of the Navy in a variety of ways including interactive exhibits, photographs, video, statues, and a small research library. The perimeter of the center is surrounded by beautiful fountains, benches, flags, and a map of the world inscribed in the pavement.

Korean War Memorial *(above and right)*

The Korean War Memorial commemorates the lives lost during the war. The memorial features 19 stainless steel statues that represent the different ethnicities and branches of military involved in the war. The memorial also features a 164-foot-long mural of over 2,400 photographs of the Korean War.

Grand Army of the Republic *(opposite)*

The Grand Army of the Republic is recognized as the first organized advocacy group in American politics. The fraternal organization lobbied Congress to establish pensions for veterans and voting rights for black veterans. The monument is dedicated to its founder, Dr. Benjamin F. Stephenson.

Vietnam Veterans Memorial
(above and opposite)

The Vietnam Veterans Memorial is etched with the names of the more than 58,000 men and women who lost their lives during the war. The memorial also features a bronze statue known as *The Three Soldiers*, which depicts three men looking solemnly in the direction of the wall.

Vietnam Women's Memorial *(left)*

The Vietnam Women's Memorial features three uniformed women, named Hope, Charity and Faith (not pictured) tending to a fallen soldier. The memorial is dedicated to the women who served during the war, most of whom were nurses, and exemplifies the importance of women during times of conflict.

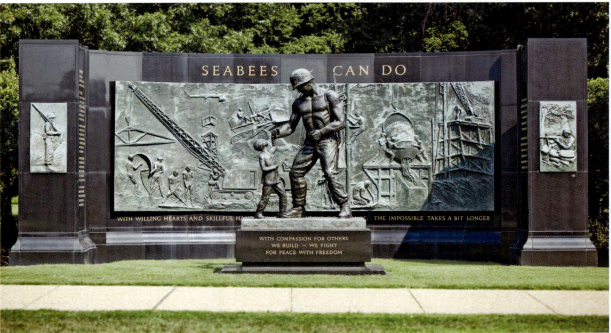

U. S. Air Force Memorial *(opposite)*

Soaring to glory, the United States Air Force Memorial depicts the majestic arc of aircraft in flight. The 270-foot-tall sculpture commemorates the men and women who have served, and continue to serve, the United States Air Force and its heritage organizations.

Honor Guard *(top)*

Representing the Honor Guard, the soldiers add a human element to the spiraling spires of the U.S. Air Force Memorial. The memorial also features two inscriptions. The north wall displays the recipients of the Air Force Medal of Honor while the south wall displays the core values of the U.S. Air Force.

Seabees Memorial *(bottom)*

The Seabees helped build and defend combat bases during times of war. Sculpted by Felix de Weldon, a former Seabee member, the memorial features a mural that depicts the many missions conducted by Seabees around the world as well as symbolizes the humanitarian aid provided by them.

Tomb of the Unknown Soldier
(top and bottom)

At the Tomb of the Unknown Soldier, one soldier stands guard to protect the tomb. In order to relieve a soldier from duty, a meticulous routine is performed during the Changing of the Guard. The Changing of the Guard occurs every half hour during the summer and every hour during the winter.

John Fitzgerald Kennedy Grave *(opposite)*

Recognized as one of the most visited sites at Arlington National Cemetery, the grave of President John F. Kennedy, who is buried with his wife and two children, is marked with an eternal flame. Robert F. Kennedy and Edward M. Kennedy are also buried at the cemetery.

Arlington National Cemetery

Spanning across 624 acres, the Arlington National Cemetery is the final resting place for those who lost their lives in battle. In addition to the somber stone memorials, there are 36 trees planted in tribute to Medal of Honor recipients. Family members may also plant a tree in memory of a loved one.

Arlington Memorial Bridge

Listed on the National Register of Historic Places, the Arlington Memorial Bridge features a neoclassical design and is decorated with monumental statues. In addition to providing a way to the cemetery, the bridge connects the Lincoln Memorial and the Arlington House, home to the Robert E. Lee Memorial.

Arlington Memorial Bridge *(above)*

Completed in 1932 after 46 years of delays, the low, neo-classical bridge is considered to be Washington, D.C.'s most beautiful bridge. Nine broad arches cross the Potomac River linking the Rock Creek Parkway and George Washington Parkway. Pedestrians enjoy striking views of the Mall and Arlington Cemetery.

Gilded Statues *(left and opposite)*

Seventeen-foot-tall gilded neoclassical statues stand guard on opposite ends of the bridge. Known as *Arts of War*, the sculptures *Valor* and *Sacrifice* flank the eastern end of the bridge. The western end features sculptures *Music and Harvest* and *Aspiration and Literature*, and together they are known as *Arts of Peace*.

Ripley Center

Located near the Smithsonian Castle, the copper domed S. Dillon Ripley Center is home to the Smithsonian Associates, Discovery Theater, and the Smithsonian Traveling Exhibition Service. The building also features a small conference center and meeting rooms with most of its facilities located underground.

Smithsonian Castle

D.C.'s most popular destination, the Castle is the first building in the suite of Smithsonian museums. It features a combination of late Romanesque architecture and Gothic motifs. The Smithsonian Castle was once home to all operations of the museum. Currently it is home to the Smithsonian Information Center and administrative offices.

National Museum of Natural History

Administered by the Smithsonian Institute, the Natural History Museum open in 1910 and is recognized as the most visited natural history museum in the world. In addition to interactive exhibits, the museum offers a variety of educational programs and supports significant scientific research around the world.

African Elephant

Unveiled in 1959 and the centerpiece of the rotunda is an African bush elephant. The museum features more than 126 million specimens including plants, fossils, minerals, cultural artifacts, animals, and meteorites. Popular exhibits include the Hope Diamond and Dinosaurs/Hall of Paleobiology.

The Space Mural: A Cosmic View *(above)*

Artist Robert McCall's mural of NASA's *Apollo 11* landing on the moon hangs in the south lobby of the National Air and Space Museum. The museum features the world's largest collection of aviation and space artifacts and is home to the Center for Earth and Planetary Studies.

Space Race Exhibit *(right)*

Exhibited side by side, The National Air and Space Museum features a variety of decommissioned missiles detailing the US and Soviet's race to the moon, which began shortly after WWII. Included in the exhibit is a Minuteman III, Viking, Scout-D, WAC Corporal, V-2, and V-1, a cruise missile known as a "buzz bomb."

National Air and Space Museum *(opposite)*

The museum boasts a collection of more than 30,000 aviation artifacts and 9,000 space objects including the 1903 *Wright Flyer*, World War II American and German aviation, military unmanned aerial vehicles, and lunar exploration vehicles. Recognized as the largest museum in the Smithsonian collection, it welcomes more than 8 million visitors annually.

National Portrait Gallery (above)

A part of the Smithsonian Institution, the gallery's art collection focuses on famous Americans including Frederick Douglass, Colin Powell, and Charlie Chaplin. Popular permanent exhibits include *America's Presidents* and *American Origins*—a gallery spanning major milestones from the 1600s to the 1900s.

Courtyard Café (opposite)

The gallery offers a variety of guest services including a gift shop and a café, which features a beautiful canopy courtesy of the Robert and Arlene Kogod Courtyard. Enjoy fresh and seasonal gourmet dining, including soups, salads, drinks, Mediterranean-inspired dishes and delicious desserts.

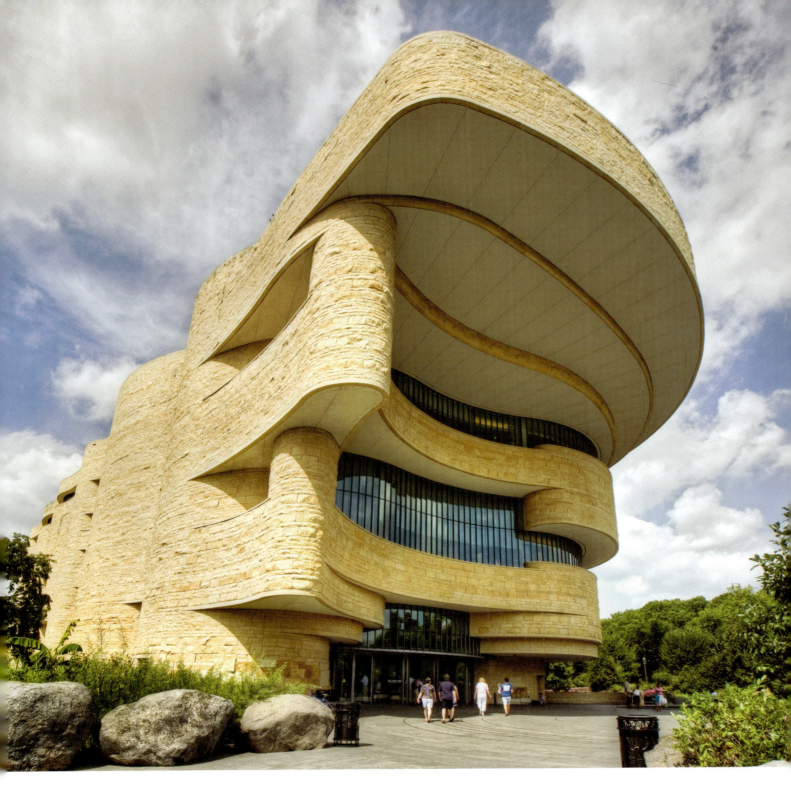

National American History Museum
(opposite, top)

Devoted to preserving the social, cultural, technological, and political heritage of the U.S., the museum houses historical artifacts such as the Star-Spangled Banner, George Washington's uniform, former first lady ball gowns, and even Dorothy's ruby red shoes from The Wonderful Wizard of Oz.

Southern 1401 Locomotive
(opposite, bottom)

Located on the first floor, the America on the Move exhibit features more than 340 objects pertaining to the transportation history of the United States. Notable items include a 1903 Winton, known as the first car driven across the country, and the 1926, green and silver Southern Railway 1401.

American Indian Museum (above)

Part of the Smithsonian Institution, the museum features an expansive collection of Native American artifacts including photographs, paintings, clothing, weaponry, pottery, and more. Notable items include Geronimo's rifle and a wall of gold objects. The museum also features a café with a Native-inspired menu.

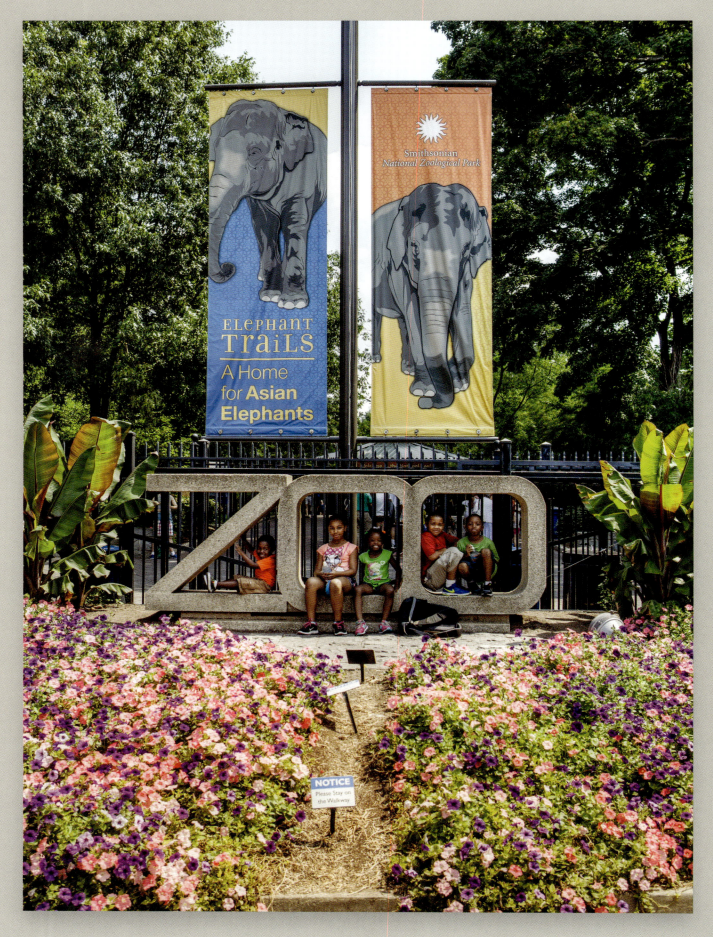

National Zoological Park *(opposite)*

Established in 1889 and recognized as one of the oldest zoos in the country, the first inhabitants of the zoo were the 185 animals under the care of the zoo's founder, William Temple Hornaday. Today, the zoo has become a leader in the protection of endangered species from around the world.

Zoo Residents *(top and bottom)*

The 163-acre National Zoo features more than 2,000 animals and 400 different species are exhibited including big cats, birds, amphibians, reptiles, small mammals, aquatic animals, insects, and more. Popular exhibits included the *Reptile Discovery Center and Great Cats*.

Hirshhorn Museum

With a focus on art made within the last 50 years, this modern art museum features the works of many well-known artists such as Pablo Picasso, Henri Matisse, and Mary Cassatt. The unique design of the museum includes an open cylinder with a large fountain located in the center.

Sculpture Garden

In addition to showcasing the world's greatest modern and contemporary art collection, the museum is also home to an extensive sculpture garden, which includes Juan Muñoz's *Last Conversation Piece* (pictured) as well as works from Auguste Rodin, Jeff Koons, and David Smith.

Renwick Gallery *(opposite, top)*

Known as the American Louvre at the time it was built, the Renwick Gallery displays contemporary American arts and crafts from the 19th, 20th and 21st centuries. The gallery also hosts Handi-hour, which combines all-you-can-craft activities with craft beer, live music, and scavenger hunts.

Freer Gallery of Art *(opposite, bottom)*

Spanning more than 6,000 years of history, the Freer Gallery features more than 26,000 artworks, sculptures, pottery, and ancient artifacts from all over the world including Asia and the Middle East. It also hosts a variety of events including films, performing arts, talks and lectures, workshops, galas, and symposiums.

National Museum of African Art *(above)*

Home to more than 9,000 artifacts, the National Museum of African Art features a wide variety of collections including sculptures, jewelry, musical instruments, textiles, ceramics, paintings, and photographs and hosts a variety of interactive programs including tours, films, and artist events.

MLK Memorial

Dedicated to the most iconic figure of the civil rights movement, the Martin Luther King, Jr. Memorial is located near the Lincoln Memorial, where Dr. King delivered his *I Have a Dream* speech. The address of the memorial, 1964 Independence Avenue, pays homage to the year the Civil Rights Act became law.

Stone of Hope (above)

Located on four acres, visitors pass between the *Mountain of Despair* to reach a 30-foot-tall likeness of Martin Luther King, Jr. carved into the *Stone of Hope*. The memorial includes a 450-foot-long wall inscribed with excerpts from Dr. King's speeches and sermons.

Cherry Blossoms at Sunrise (pages 62 – 63)

The beauty of Washington, D.C. flourishes with blossoming cherry trees along the Tidal Basin at sunrise. A second gift of more than 3,800 cherry trees from the Japanese government was received in 1965, of which many were planted on the grounds of the Washington Monument.

Franklin Delano Roosevelt Memorial

Depicting notable moments throughout his presidential term, the FDR Memorial consists of four open rooms —one for each of his terms in office. Robert Graham's statue of Roosevelt sitting in a wheel chair acknowledges FDR's significant disability experience that forged his leadership qualities and enabled him to lead our nation.

Fala

Many of the sculptures throughout the park were inspired by photographs taken throughout FDR's presidency, including one where the former president sits beside his beloved dog Fala. Other sculptures include a bronze statue of his wife, scenes from the Great Depression, and FDR's funeral procession.

Albert Einstein Memorial *(above and left)*

Located at the National Academy of Sciences, the Albert Einstein Memorial pays homage to the great scientist and documents his most famous achievements including the photoelectric effect, the general relativity theory, and equivalence of energy and matter. Three of his quotations are also inscribed in the memorial.

Japanese American Patriotism Memorial

Featuring two cranes wrapped in barbed wire, the memorial commemorates the valiant effort and patriotism of Japanese Americans during World War II. The symbolic sculpture represents the importance of working together in order to break free from prejudice and struggle to become a unified and strong country.

Stars

The *Dupont Circle Fountain* is made of three allegorical figures representing the Wind, the Sea, and the Stars (pictured). Completed in 1920 by famed sculptor, Daniel Chester French, it is dedicated in memory of one of the most famous naval figures of the Civil War, Rear Admiral Samuel Francis Du Pont.

Mahatma Gandhi Memorial

Recognized as the father of India, the statue memorializes Gandhi's protest against the salt tax in 1930. The sculpture also pays tribute to the leader's many marches for civil rights for everyone around the world. Located near Dupont Circle, the statue was a gift from the Indian Council for Cultural Relations.

Kennedy Center (above and right)

Home to approximately 2,000 performances a year, the John F. Kennedy Center for the Performing Arts presents the best local, national, and international performing artists. Productions at the performing arts center include world class ballets, opera, theater, symphonies, orchestras, and a variety of musical styles including jazz, world, and folk.

Grand Foyer (opposite)

The interior of the performing arts center features a beautiful grand foyer with 16 hand-blown Orrefors crystal chandeliers, the Hall of States, and the Hall of Nations. Robert Berks' 3,000 pound, eight-foot-tall bronze bust of President Kennedy is located in the center of the hall.

United States Botanic Garden

Established in 1820, the mission of the Botanic Garden is to show the importance and value of plants. The facility features a variety of exhibits and environments, a glass-enclosed conservatory, rose and butterfly gardens, an amphitheater, and a regional garden.

Rose Garden

Meandering pathways lead to the Rose Garden, which includes every type of America's national flower. Using organic methods, this ongoing experiment showcases old garden roses, modern hybrids, miniatures and climbers, as well as shrub and species roses. Tours, educational programs, and events are free of charge.

National Archives *(above)*

Known as the nation's record keeper, the National Archives and Records Administration houses many important historical documents including the Declaration of Independence, the Constitution, and the Bill of Rights. Other notable documents include the Emancipation Proclamation and a copy of the 1297 Magna Carta.

Study the Past *(opposite)*

Located near the Pennsylvania Avenue entrance are two sculptures—one of a woman (not shown) representing the future and one of a man representing the past. *Past* and *Future* sit on pedestals with the following words inscribed, "Study the Past" and "What is Past is Prologue," respectively.

Neptune Fountain *(above)*

Located at the Library of Congress, the lavishly beautiful *Neptune Fountain* depicts the Roman god of the sea sitting on a bed of rocks while two minor sea gods summon the water deities. The fountain also features a variety of sea creatures including wild sea horses, nymphs, sea monsters, frogs, and turtles.

Great Hall *(right and opposite)*

Completed in 1897 and recognized as the oldest federal cultural institution in the country, the Library of Congress is one of the two largest libraries in the world. Featured in the Great Hall are two marble staircases topped with bronze female figures.

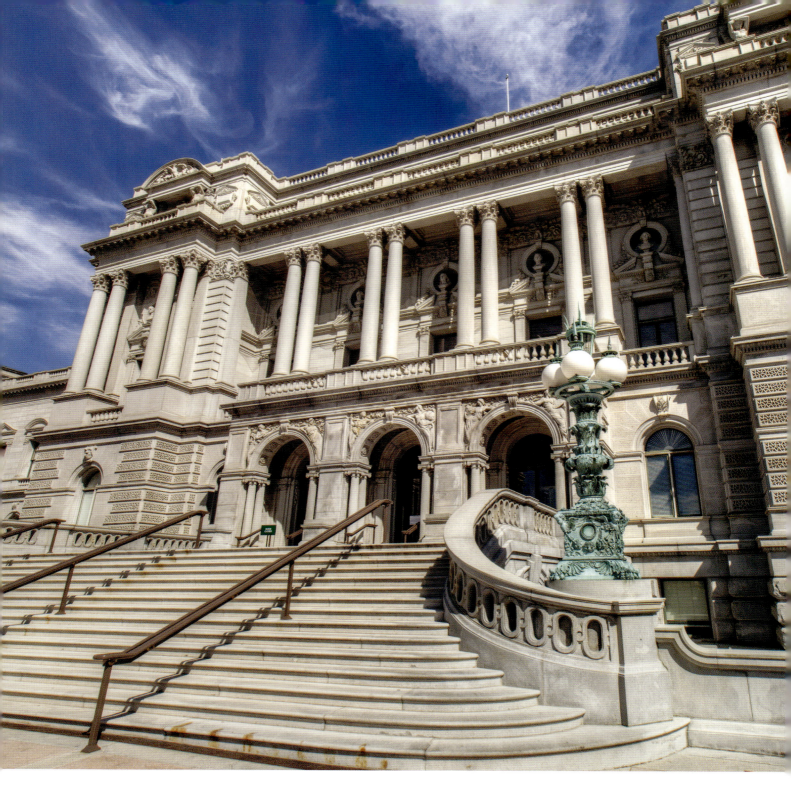

Jefferson Building

Spread across four buildings, the Thomas Jefferson Building of the Library of Congress features Italian Renaissance architecture as well as sculptures and painted decorations from more than 50 American artists. Located in front of the second story windows are the busts of nine great men.

Main Entrance

Located along the granite railings of the front entranceway are two elaborate bronze candelabras topped with clusters of electric lamps. The theatrical and heavily-ornamented style is apparent throughout the facility through the use of costly materials, including 15 varieties of marble and other lavish materials.

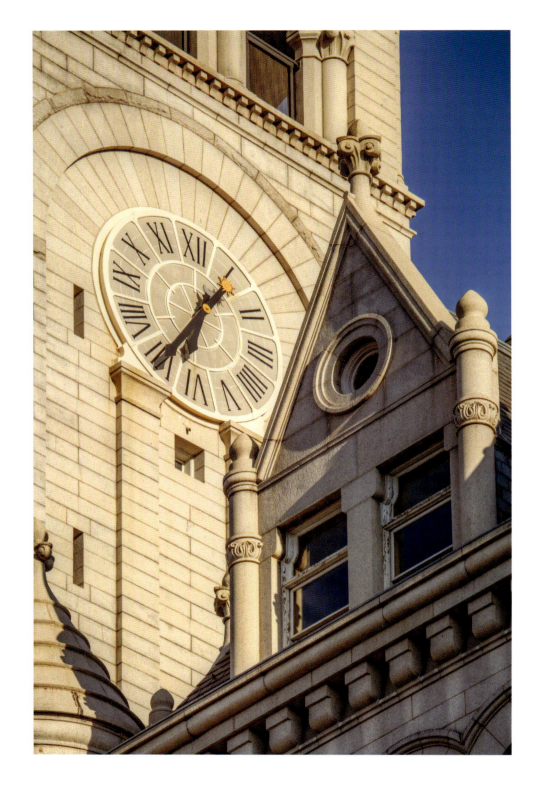

Old Post Office *(above and opposite)*

One of D.C.'s most popular attractions, the Old Post Office Pavilion features sweeping views of the city from its 315 foot clock tower. The tower is also home to the official United States Bells of Congress, which rings every Thursday evening and for special occasions courtesy of the Washington Ringing Society.

War

Originally known as the State, War and Navy Building, the Eisenhower Executive Office Building is topped with *War*, a medieval suit of armor sculpture with an American eagle resting on top of the helmet. Completed in 1884, artist Richard von Ezdorf was also the building's chief draftsman and designer.

Eisenhower Executive Office Building

Located next to the White House, the Eisenhower Executive Office Building features cast iron, granite and slate architecture and is considered one of the best examples of French Second Empire architecture in the country. It houses offices for White House staff and has been the scene of many historic events.

Cannon House (opposite)

Built to help relieve overcrowding at the U.S. Capitol, the Cannon House Office Building is the oldest congressional building in D.C. Featuring the Beaux Arts style of architecture, the rotunda is comprised of 18 Corinthian columns, a glazed oculus, twin marble staircases, and a beautifully detailed ceiling.

Clinton Federal Building (above)

Originally known as the New Post Office Building, the Clinton Federal Building houses the headquarters of the Environmental Protection Agency. Designed with the Classical Revival architecture, the building features monumental columns, porticos, and arched openings as well as two grand curving facades.

Wilson Building (above)

Home of the D.C. Mayor and Council, the original location of the Wilson Building was once a streetcar power station. The exterior of the building resembles the Beaux Arts architecture evident throughout the city. Composed of granite and marble, the top floor features sculptures of heroic figures.

EPA Building (opposite)

Built using limestone and granite, the neoclassical building features Classic Revival architecture with its two large semicircles constructed back to back with side wings extending out from each side. Each elevation of the exterior displays a different combination of columns, porticos, and arched openings.

Union Station Plaza *(above)*

Modeled after the Baths of Caracalla and Diocletian and the Arch of Rome, Union Station set the architectural tone of many buildings in D.C. The station's centerpiece is the 1912 *Columbus Fountain*. Flanked by a Native American and an elderly man, Columbus looks beyond a winged figurehead representing the observation of discovery.

Federal Trade Commission
(right and opposite)

Located on a triangular piece of land, the architecture of the building features elements of Classical Revival architecture including columns, a portico, and open-air arcaded space. Two nearly identical sculptures, *Man Controlling Trade*, are located outside the eastern entrance of the building.

Symbols of Justice *(above and left)*

Atop the staircase leading to the Supreme Court are James Earl Frazer's two stern figures, *Contemplation of Justice* (above) and a male figure known as *Guardian* or *Authority of Law*. Two bronze-based flagpoles, located on either end of the plaza, are decorated with child figures and numerous symbols of justice.

Supreme Court *(opposite)*

Conceived as a temple of justice, the plaza leading to the Supreme Court building contains two fountain pools and is paved with gray and white marble patterned squares as seen at the Roman Parthenon. Completed in 1935, the architrave above the 16 columns is inscribed with, "Equal Justice Under Law."

Corcoran Gallery of Art *(above and left)*

With the largest privately-owned collection in D.C., the gallery features the work of well-known artists including Pablo Picasso, Claude Monet, and Rembrandt. The building, featuring prevalent Beaux Arts style architecture, has recently undergone restoration to protect the intricately designed exterior from the elements.

National Building Museum

With 75-foot-tall Corinthian columns and a 1,200-foot-long terra cotta frieze, the interior and exterior of the National Building Museum is awe inspiring. Devoted to the history and impact of buildings and architecture, the museum also features more than 230 busts and an arcade with 72 Doric and Ionic-style columns.

National Headquarters (above)

Known as the "marble palace," the American Red Cross houses historic works of art and artifacts from many well-known artists. The building is also known for its beautiful three-paneled Tiffany window collection, located in the Board of Governors Hall, designed and constructed by Louis Comfort Tiffany.

Motherland (opposite)

The grounds of the American Red Cross building feature a collection of sculptures, including *Motherland*, presented by the people of Armenia. The sculpture is a visual representation of appreciation for the aid the country received when a 7.2 magnitude earthquake hit Armenia in 1988.

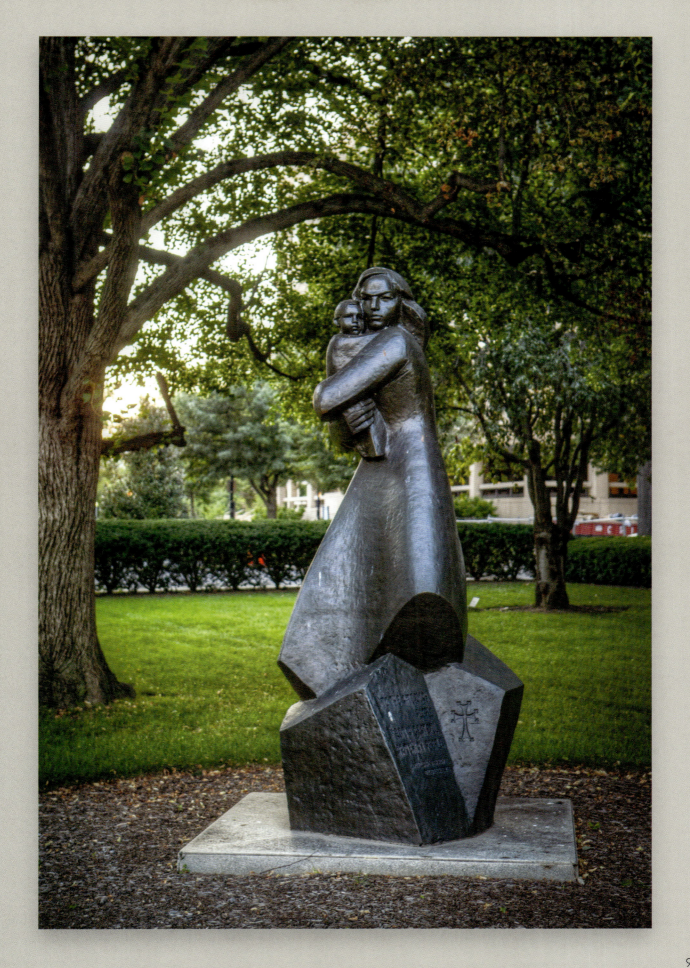

Ulysses S. Grant Memorial (opposite)

Towering 44 feet above the ground and guarded by four impressive bronze lions is the 1901 Ulysses S. Grant Memorial. Sitting on a base made of white Vermont marble and located in Union Square, the sculpture faces Grant's wartime president, Abraham Lincoln.

Federal Reserve Building (above)

Named for former chairman of the Federal Reserve, the building was constructed so that the Federal Reserve and its Board of Governors would work together in one building. Designed with the Beaux-Arts architecture, the property also features sculptures, mantel ornaments, and a large map of the U.S. in its Board Room.

Lafayette Statue (top)

Encompassing 7 acres, Lafayette Square offers visitors well-manicured grounds, walkways, fountains and sculptures, including Marquis de Lafayette and Andrew Jackson on horseback as well as other Revolutionary War heroes. The square also features numerous homes of historical figures including Dolley Madison, Stephen Decatur, Henry Adams, and John Hay.

Calvary Charge (bottom)

Known as the *Calvary Charge*, the statue is part of a three statue memorial for Ulysses S. Grant. The collection of statues pays homage to the former president who was best known for being a strategic commander in chief and playing a key role in the surrender of Robert E. Lee.

Sheridan Circle (opposite)

Named after the Union General of the Civil War, the memorial pays tribute to the man who contributed to the defeat of confederate forces at Appomattox. Sheridan was also instrumental in the development of Yellowstone National Park. Sheridan Circle is home to numerous foreign embassies and beautiful homes.

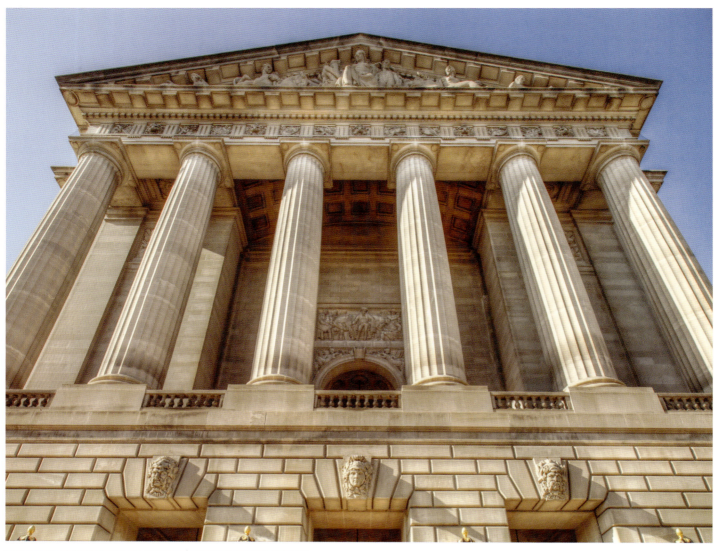

Mellon Auditorium (above)

Many numerous historical events took place at the auditorium including the reinstitution of the draft in 1940, the signing of the North Atlantic Treaty in 1949, and the signing of the North American Free Trade Agreement. Today, it is used to host galas, weddings, conferences, corporate functions, and other events.

Architecture Detail (left and opposite)

Designed by Arthur Brown Jr., the auditorium features 20-foot-tall arched entrances, gilded and burnished aluminum detail, fluted Roman Doric columns, and a gorgeously detailed pediment titled *Columbia* by Edgar Walter, which symbolizes the country, national defense, and national resources.

Ronald Reagan Building (above)

Currently the largest structure in D.C., the building houses both government and private trade-related businesses. The facility also includes a premier conference and event center, shops, restaurants and concierge services as well as an amphitheater where the infamous satire *Capitol Steps* is performed year-round.

Thomas Circle (opposite)

Located in the center of the circle, the statue pays tribute to Union General George Henry Thomas who played a key role in a handful of battles including the Battle of Chickamauga and the Battle of Chattanooga. Thomas Circle also features well-manicured lawns, bike lanes, and a pedestrian walkway.

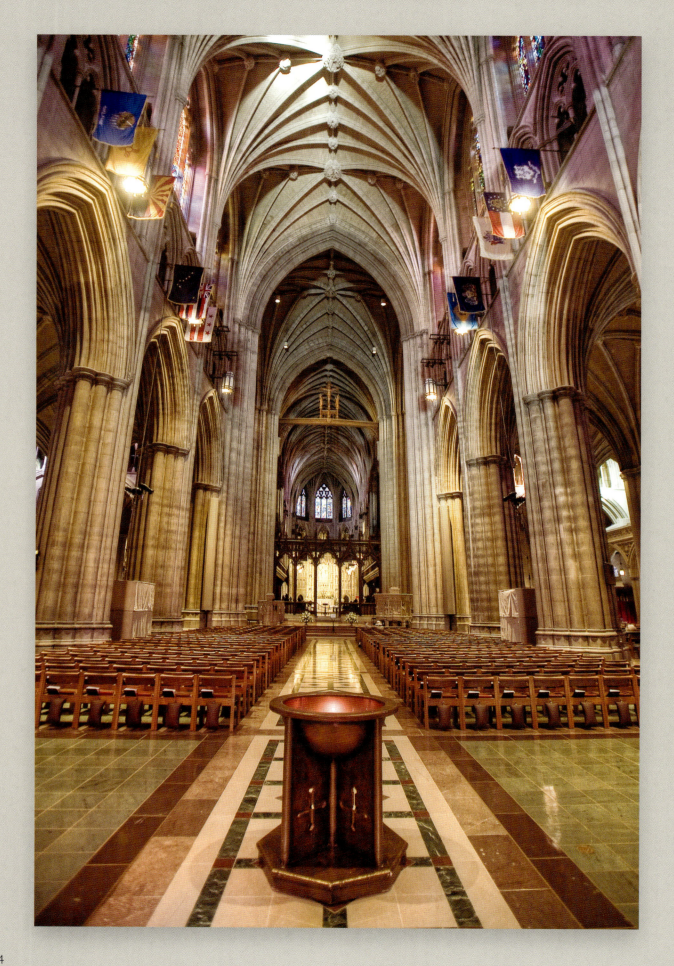

National Cathedral Interior *(opposite)*

Completed 83 years to the day after its inception, the Washington National Cathedral welcomes more than 700,000 visitors each year and boasts 215 stained glass windows, with more than 10,500 pieces of stained glass encompassing the beautiful west rose window.

National Cathedral *(above)*

Recognized as the sixth largest cathedral in the world and the second largest in the United States, the cathedral is located on 57 acres and contains 53 bells, 112 gargoyles, and more than 1,500 pieces of needlepoint. The central tower stands 676 feet above sea level, the highest point in Washington, D.C.

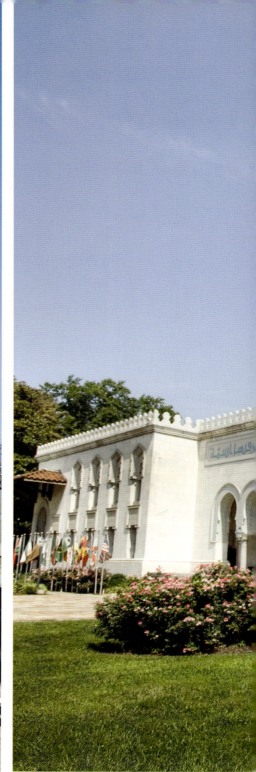

St. John's Church

Known as the "Church of the Presidents," every president since James Madison has attended services at St. John's Church. A designated pew, number 54, is available for the President to use should they wish to worship at the church. Completed in 1816, Paul Revere's foundry cast the church's bell in 1822.

Islamic Center

Established to promote a better understanding of Islam in the U.S., the center provides information and literature to increase awareness and knowledge of the religion. The center also features a research center, library, and classrooms. The building was designed by Italian architect Mario Rossi and completed in 1957.

Basilica of the National Shrine
(above and opposite)

The 329-foot-tall campanile and cobalt blue dome define the Basilica of the National Shrine. Housing 70 chapels, the basilica boasts the largest collection of contemporary ecclesiastical art in the world, including the giant mosaic *Christ in Majesty* by John de Rosen.

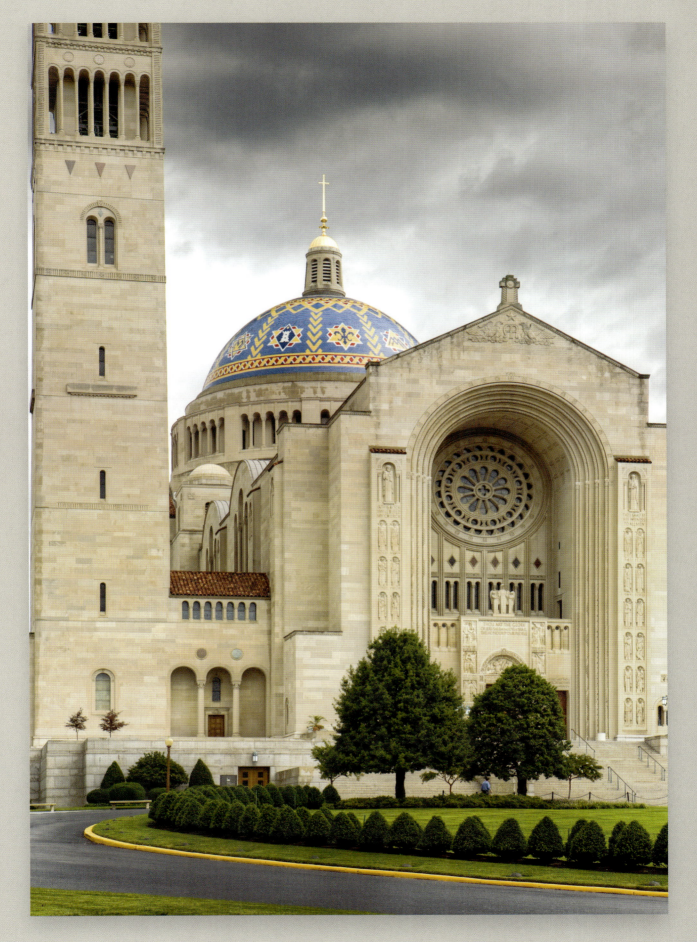

Willard Hotel *(opposite)*

Renowned as the Crown Jewel of Pennsylvania Avenue, the hotel has hosted almost every U.S. president since 1853. The larger suites of the hotel are named after our country's founding fathers. Other notable guests from the past include Charles Dickens, Buffalo Bill, Dr. Martin Luther King, Jr., and P.T. Barnum.

Dumbarton Bridge *(above)*

A gentle curving bridge connects Georgetown and Dupont Circle. Also known as Buffalo Bridge and the Q Street Bridge, its entrances are adorned with four bronze buffalo statues by Alexander Proctor. Completed in 1915, its five large arches are decorated with 56 carved sandstone heads of Kicking Bear, a Sioux Chief.

International Spy Museum *(above and right)*

The only public museum devoted to the world of espionage, the museum features interactive exhibits, spy experiences, and the largest collection of international spy artifacts on display. The museum also demonstrates the important role spies have played in uncovering major events throughout history.

Madame Tussauds *(opposite)*

A major tourist attraction, the D.C. branch of the popular wax museum features wax replicas of a wide variety of politicians, historical figures, sports figures and celebrities including Rosa Parks, Johnny Depp, and Babe Ruth. The museum also offers a behind-the-scenes look into the production of modern day wax figures.

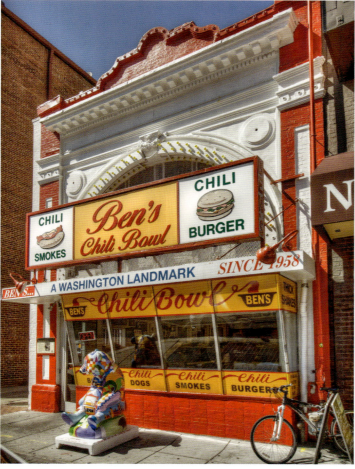

Friendship Archway (above)

Chinatown's Friendship Arch welcomes visitors on H Street. Decorated with 23-karat gold, over 7,000 glazed tiles, and 272 carved and painted dragons, the archway mirrors the style of the Ming and Qing dynasties. This small, historic neighborhood offers authentic Chinese restaurants and shops.

Ben's Chili Bowl (left)

A D.C. institution, many celebrities and politicians have been spotted eating at "the Bowl." The restaurant has received numerous awards and accolades, been published in numerous press outlets, and has been featured on many popular shows including *Oprah*, *Good Morning America*, and *Man vs. Food*.

Calvary Baptist Church (opposite)

Renowned as the founding church of the Northern Baptist Convention, Calvary Baptist Church's recognizable red brick exterior was builder Adolf Cluss' favorite material. Located in the Penn Quarter and completed in 1866, it offers a variety of services including English classes, Sunday school, and special musical events.

Epoch (above)

Albert Paley's *Epoch*, a large multi-colored metal sculpture, is located in downtown D.C., near the National Portrait Gallery. D.C. is also home to a vibrant—and delicious—restaurant scene. From fast food to luxurious five-course meals, visitors will find a variety of cuisines to choose from including French, Greek, Turkish, Lebanese, Asian, Italian and others.

Gallery Place (opposite)

Downtown's Gallery Place features residential complexes, shopping, restaurants, businesses, and entertainment in one hip neighborhood. Located near Chinatown and the Verizon Center, the always-buzzing-with people destination is also home to the Lucky Strike bowling alley and Regal Cinemas.

Downtown

The U.S. Capitol is the center point which separates Washington, D.C. into its four quadrants. It is believed that the original city plan developed by Pierre Charles L'Enfant in 1791, and thus presented to George Washington, has been preserved in the Library of Congress.

Embassy Row

D.C. is home to more than 175 foreign embassies, residences and cultural centers, many of which exist on Embassy Row, located along Massachusetts Avenue Northwest. Numerous embassies offer a variety of events to the public including educational programs, lectures, exhibitions, concerts, and other special events.

Foreign Flags

Each year the Embassy Series organization creates a schedule of events that highlight the culture and heritage of participating embassies. Each event features a musical production followed by a reception at the selected embassy. These events help encourage interaction with artists as well as the foreign diplomatic community.

Red Door *(opposite)*

Rich in character, Dupont Circle constitutes two primary styles of residences—palatial mansions and freestanding homes, and multiple-story rowhouses. Many of the homes feature unique colors, styles, embellishments and architecture. To add to the charm, the neighborhood also boasts brick sidewalks and tree-lined streets.

Dupont Circle *(left and right)*

Originally built from the 1880s, many of the homes located in Dupont Circle feature variations of styles and architecture including Queen Anne, Richardson Revival, Renaissance, and Georgian Revival. The most impressive series of rowhouses with different styles can be found along the 2000 block of Hillyer Place.

Adams Morgan Neighborhood
(top and bottom)

A popular destination for the younger crowd, Adams Morgan features a variety of independently owned businesses, restaurants, and entertainment venues. A popular destination is Madam's Organ, a clever play on words of the neighborhood's name.

Vibrant Neighborhood *(opposite)*

The vibrancy found on 18th street, known as the main drag in Adams Morgan, spills into nearby neighborhoods. Recognized as a culturally diverse community, visitors are often drawn to the variety of international shops as well as delectable ethnic cuisine that can be found throughout the neighborhood.

Georgetown University
(above and opposite, top)

Founded 1789 and the oldest Jesuit and Christian university in the U.S., Georgetown University is an internationally recognized research facility. Founded by John Carroll, the first Catholic bishop of the U.S., its design is based on the Collegiate Gothic and Georgian brick architectural styles.

Archbishop John Carroll Statue *(right)*

Founder of Georgetown University, a statue of Archbishop John Carroll sits in front of Healy Hall. Sculpted by Jerome Connor and completed in 1912, the founder's chair is over a stack of books representing the importance of religion, education, and learning.

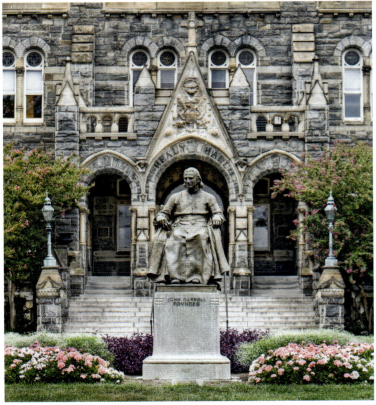

Rowing on the Potomac (top)

A popular place for sport and leisure activities, the Potomac River was once considered a major shipping route. As the river began to grow shallower, larger ships had a difficult time coming to port. Today, the river is now used for recreational purposes and to provide drinking water for D.C. residents.

C&O Canal (bottom)

During the 19th and 20th centuries the canal helped provide opportunities and growth to nearby cities and towns. Damage caused by large floods led to the gradual decline of use for the canal. Today, the canal offers a gorgeous backdrop and peaceful respite from the hustle and bustle of city life.

Gold-Leafed Dome (opposite)

A familiar landmark in the heart of downtown Georgetown, the gold-domed building formerly housed D.C.-based Riggs Bank. In 2005, the bank merged with PNC Financial Services, who currently resides in the building.

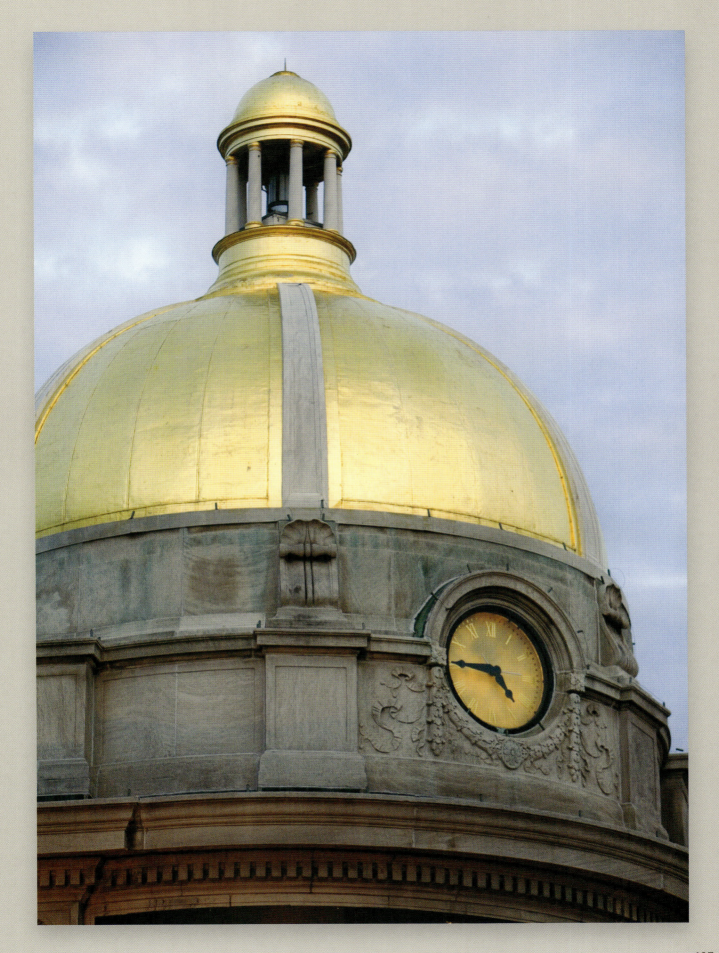

Randy Santos

Randy Santos is a photographer whose artistic vision and unique personal perspective on the world around him has established him as one of Washington, D.C.'s preeminent photographers.

A native Washingtonian with over 30 years of photographic experience, Randy's work reflects his passion and drive for creative self-expression, a mastery of the medium of photography, and his love for the architectural beauty and history found in his hometown.

Randy's distinctive work is regularly featured in art installations, corporate and hospitality environments, government facilities, and innumerable print and electronic media worldwide.

In addition to being an artist, Randy is also a husband and father. Randy has established a business model that enables him to make family life a priority while enjoying the aesthetic and personal fulfillment that his work brings.

To see more of Randy's work or to purchase photographs found in this book, please visit www.dcstockphotos.com.

Susan Diranian

Born and raised in the Washington, D.C. area, Susan Diranian is a freelance writer and editor. Her work has appeared in numerous local and national publications including *USA Today*, the *Nest*, *CBS Washington* and the *Examiner*. Topics that she covers include relationships, travel, beauty, and health.

Susan also owns and operates Review my Paper, a small business that provides writing and editing support, guidance, and advice for a variety of documents. She currently resides in the D.C. area with her husband.